Fly Without a Shadow

Meditations on Oneness

Edited by Dr Edwin Pugh

First edition (CreateSpace Publication 2017)

e-mail: **enquiries@movements.me.uk**

websites: **www.movements.me.uk**

www.transformhealthcarecambodia.org.uk

Published by Sharp Edge Publishing - 'Movements' 2017

'The suffering of Cambodia has been deep.

From this suffering comes great compassion.

Great compassion makes a peaceful heart.

A peaceful heart makes a peaceful person.

A peaceful person makes a peaceful family.

A peaceful family makes a peaceful community.

A peaceful community makes a peaceful nation.

And a peaceful nation makes a peaceful world.

May all beings live in happiness and peace'.

Teaching of Maha Ghosananda (Known as the Ghandi of Cambodia)

Context

The writer is a man approaching the later stages of his life. He has dedicated his life to serving the poorest of the poor. The first portion of service was in ghettos in the USA. The last 25 plus years have been with the poor in Cambodia. He has seen and experienced first-hand the results of abject poverty, war and its aftermath.

The writer's life remains one of service for his God who he calls, 'I am who am'. In Cambodia he lives with the Buddhist monks. He has literally walked with the venerable Maha Ghosananda, known as the 'Ghandi of Cambodia', on Dhammayietra *(peace walks)* across a war torn Cambodia. He has embraced teachings of Sufi described in the Koran as a servant of God bringing divine love and wisdom into the world. He has sought to follow God and to hear 'I am who am' in understanding humanity and our part in relieving suffering.

Written during June and July 2015, these are a deeply spiritual collection of meditations presented in their chronological order. They are written from the heart. They are written from deep experience. They are a reflection of the soul of one who seeks God with all of his being.

Foreword

In the silence of each very early morning the writer of this collection of meditations begins his day spending time before his God. He calls his God, 'I am who am'.
It is a precious time. A time of recognising that 'I am who am' is love. A time of hearing 'I am who am's words in the silence.

A time of being 'one' with 'I am who am'.

Following the meditation he writes. The thoughts and words flow spontaneously. They are from the heart, even from the soul. They are not drafted or crafted. Like an impressionist painter, 'en plein', capturing the moment, the emotion and the vibrancy - he uses words not paint to address his spiritual canvas.

His words are not divorced from reality. They acknowledge the temporary reality of the world as we see it today. They point to the eternal reality of life with and in God. The words point to a path where those that walk can have peace and purpose in their lives on earth at one with themselves, each other and their God.

Introduction

This is a collection of meditations about some of life's fundamental philosophical questions:

Why am I here?
Why me?
What is my purpose?
What is my value?
What is death?
How should I love?

It is not a book about religion. I hope it will be of interest to those both with and without a faith but who philosophically question the purpose of life.

These are meditations to be approached with a mind focused on seeking inner truths. They require a willing heart and mind to approach the silence of self freed from worldly considerations. For the writer, he is approaching his God to experience oneness with Him and to hear His voice in the silence.

My suggestion would be to meditate on one of the writings daily and to follow them chronologically in the sequence they were written. Each meditation builds upon the previous and influences the next.
My hope is that these words will speak to you, the reader (or hearer), to bring some peace and purpose in your life. I hope they will help you see there is an existential reality beyond the reality of the world you know and that you have a place and purpose in both - in love.

Table of Contents

1. Fly Without a Shadow

After all the words be spoken
After all the songs be sung
I am who am dwells in the silence
In the nothingness of love

Come sit, walk
Dwell in the silence of oneness
Is one
In love

Silence is the language
The language of the heart
It is within the silence
I am who am's word imparts
I am who am's word
Is imprinted upon the heart

Silence is the only word
That need be spoken
Silence is the sound of a love
Being broken wide open

Love is the language
Spoken in the silence of the heart
A silent love is the love
I am who am imparts

I am who am's imprint
Is upon the human heart
Touch the imprint
Know I am who am's heart

The heart of oneness
The heart of love
Oneness
Is one
In love

The power of oneness
The power of one
Is to be found only in love
I am who am is only
Only love

Love is a power
Love is one
Now walk in the silence
Of only, only love

Let love be the light
Which shines in the eye
I am who am is
I am who teaches how to fly

To fly without a shadow
To sing without an echo
To love silently
Without leaving a trace
Now love with I am who am's fragrant grace

Let love permeate
One's place
One's faith
Let love be the light which shines in the eyes
Let love teach one
How to fly
I am who am teaches one how to fly

When one walks with only
Love within one's heart
This is the love which only
I am who am can impart

Love burns
Love soothes
Love does
Whatever is needed
To set the people free
Free to see the world
As it is meant to be

I am who am
Sets free
For all to see
Be free
I am who am free

The wonder of oneness
The wonder of one
One loves with the oneness
Of one
One loves like love

Let all one meets know
Such love in the heart
Let the love be palpable
Without obstacle or veil
Let the love shine
As one breathes in and breathes out
This love
One does not exhale

The purity of oneness
The purity of one
To love like the sun
Love like the sun
Love with the oneness of one

The words are esoteric
The reality is real
Love with the oneness
Which is real

Love with a purity
That makes all clear
I am who am loves with a oneness
Which is real

Be real!
The mother of love
The father of truth
Is what makes it real

Maha taught one to walk (1)
With two feet
Wisdom and compassion are ingredients
Of a love complete

Having one without the other
One's love is incomplete
It is wisdom and compassion
Which washes one's feet

Simple teachings to guide
One's feet as one walks along the way
Simple teachings to prevent suffering
As one walks on the path given each day

To be touched by suffering
To see it with I am who am's eyes
Purified in such love
One knows how to respond

Love me
Love me alone
And one knows
How to respond

Loving in oneness
Loving with oneness
One knows
How to respond

Oneness is one loves with wisdom and compassion
Oneness is one loves freely
Oneness is one sets one's heart
Sets one's feet free

Be faithful to the path given
Be one, be free,
Be me
I am who am

Oneness is to be found in the silence of me
I am who am
Be free
Be me freely
For in the mystery
In the miracle of that oneness
Is one
That's how it be
Now Be!

(1) - Maha - Maha Ghosananda.

2. Silence Speaks in Words of Love

Sit in the silence
Be
Sit in the silence
Free
Sit in the silence
See
The world as it is meant to be
Sit in the silence
Be

Sit in the silence
Don't try to explain to me
I am who am
Sit in the silence free

Free to move
Where the heart moves free
To walk where I am who am's feet
Carry thee

Sit in the silence
To know the path
One is to walk upon
Sit in the silence
Come
To know
I am who am's song

Sit in the silence
Before any action begins
Sit in the silence
Where one is not tainted
By the nafs and sin (1)

Sit in the silence
A place of love
And purity
The silence where one has already
Been set free

Sit in the silence
And know only me
I am who am
Sit in the silence
Be
The silence of I am who am
Me

Before a word is spoken
Before thought is formed
Before an action is taken
Before the birth
Before the storm
Silence is
Silence is

Before the pen lays its head on paper
Before the word is formed
Before the idea takes shape
Silence is
Silence is

Silence speaks in silence
Silence speaks silently
Before a word is spoken
Silence frees

Learn the voice of the heart
Before a word touches the tongue
The language of the heart
Is the silence of oneness
Is one

Silence is
The language of the circle of love
Silence speaks in and outside
Of human time
Silence speaks in words of love

A silent love is spoken
In the heart of every one of thee
Silence spoken here is
The language of the free

Free to know
Free to be
The ultimate truth
The ultimate reality
Know
Be this truth
In its earthly reality
I am who am
Frees one to see
To be

For I am who am is the ultimate reality
In the nothingness of nothingness
In the nothingness which frees
Come to see
Come to understand
The earthly realities

Come to see
From the heart of hearts
Come to perceive
From the heart of me
I am who am

Only from the heart of hearts
Can one come to truly see
Come into the silence
Come silently
Come truly see

Do not be afraid
Of the reality of me
I am who am
Free

The beauty of existence
The beauty of being
Is the beauty of me
I am who am

Don't be fooled by the aberrations
Which do not free
All created form
Is part of me
I am who am

All created form
Lives and breathes in me
I am who am
Live and breathe in me

While thou art formed as mortal human
When one lets go of form
One returns fully in me
I am who am
Spirit
Free
Oneness is one in spirit free

(1) - Nafs - are the ego or self.

3. The Miracle of Oneness

The miracle of oneness
Is the miracle of I am who am
Oneness perceives the world as one
Oneness sees oneness
Only oneness is perceived
It is oneness which frees

To be lost
In the company
Of those lost in God
Is to be lost in the oneness of one
The oneness of God

Do not be limited by the inadequacy
Of the human world
Do not be limited by the nature of man
It is a temporary reality
One is given
Be faithful to that time and space

I am who am is
A hidden treasure
Desiring to make
Oneness known
In oneness
Oneness is shown

The light of oneness
Shines brightly for those
Who walk in
I am who am's ways

Like the sun, the moon
And the stars
All reflect the light of oneness
Of One

I am who am is
A hidden treasure
Desiring to make oneness known
The light of oneness
Makes all known

In this earthly life
One is busy
About many things
Be Martha be

But it was the light of oneness
That Mary perceived in Jesus' eye
That led Jesus to say
Mary had chosen the better half

Mary learned
To listen in the silence
Mary learned how to see
And believe

Seeing this realm
With the light of oneness
Allows one to see its beauty
As well as its ugly realities

Where hatred greed and ignorance
Have taken hold
Blocking the human ability to see

The oneness
To perceive
The ultimate reality

Light confronts the darkness
By its very being
Look at the lives of those who are spiritually free
They spoke out to the darkness
Of their times and places

They willingly gave/give their lives
Within the light of love
Which allows them to see
The reality
As it is

To perceive reality
As it is meant to be
I am who am is reality
As it is meant to be

See, perceive, believe
I am's he whom I love
Is me
I am who am
Be!

In the mystery of oneness
One comes to see
To perceive
To believe

In the mystery of oneness
One comes to see
Reality as it is
To perceive reality
As it is meant to be

4. The Path into the Always

Be one
Be one
And Free
Be one
Be one
In me

Be a love
Beyond all human understanding
Be a love
Within the beloved's heart
Is standing

Oneness is a gift
Oneness is the reality
It is oneness
Which sets us free

Oneness takes one there
Oneness brings one back
Oneness keeps one
On the right track

Oneness is a state of being
Oneness is to be
In such a divine mystery
All are set free

Free to see
The world as it is
Free to be
Freely

Not a word
Slips out of the pen
Which does not speak
In the oneness of me

The light of love comes
In many shades
The language of love is silence
In its many depths

The acts of love
Are the path into the always
I am who am is
The path of always
Walk on this path
Into the always

The power of one
The power of oneness
Carries one
Into the always

Walk on walk on
Into the always
The power of the present moment
The power of the now

To Be!
Oneness is one
In the present moment
To Be!
Oneness is one in the now

Is to be
Oneness is
One in me
I am who am

I am who am is oneness
I am who am is free
Touch the oneness
Touch me
I who am free

The miracle of oneness
The miracle of now
Are no miracles at all
It is simply
The reality
In such oneness
Be free

I am who am loves
With everlasting love
I am who am gives
I am who am lives
In oneness
Is love

Oneness is one
In everlasting love
Be!
One!
Be!

5. The Walker and the Way

I am who am
Is the sunrise
I am who am is the sun
I am who am is the presence
Within each and every one
Come walk with me in the sun

I am who am is the now
I am who am comes in the present moment
Of every now
I am who am comes now

The mystery of oneness
The mystery of one
In oneness I am who am
Walks in each and every one

Walk
Walk on now
Be
Be on
The way

In oneness is one
I am who am is the walker
I am who am is the way

6. The Walk Without Legs

The silence of me
I am who am
Is
The silence of thee

For in the silence
There is no me
No thee
There is only I am who am

In silence there is only oneness
In silence there is only, 'is'
In silence there is only presence
Of the one
Of the oneness that is

In silence there is presence
In silence oneness is free
Not limited by any limitations
Of the earthly realities

In silence there is only me
I am who am

I am who am is a hidden treasure
Desiring to make myself known
I am who am is a hidden treasure
Always coming home
In the oneness of one
One comes home
Come home

In the silence of oneness
One is already home
Be!
At home
Be!
Home

In the presence of silence
In the silence of presence
I am who am
Is home

Be!
Home
I am who am 'is'
Home

In the silence of oneness
In the silence of one
I am who am is
Is home
Silence is one's home
Come home
Be home

Be!
Home in the heart of silence
Be! Home in the heart of me
I am who am
Be!
The vessel I am who am is inviting
All to be

Be! A vessel of oneness
Be! A vessel of one
Be!
Free in the oneness of one

Watch for I am who am's glimpses
Listen for I am who am's whisper
Wait for I am who am's glance
For it is I am who am
Walking in clay feet

'Watch his feet, Lord Watch His feet'
Were the words told in advance
Let one's feet walk
In the direction where one hears
I am who am's voice
Let one's feet walk

Listen for I am who am's voice
Those in the spiritual realms
Those no longer with feet of clay
Walk in the feet of others
Who still walk on the path of clay

In oneness I am who am
Walks with feet of clay
I am who am walks silently
More visibly in those who say, 'yes'

In those who consciously
Give their hearts
Over to the reality
Of oneness
In those who are able to walk more freely
Free others to learn how to walk
More freely

'Tis the walk without legs
On the path
One is invited to walk upon
'Tis the walk without legs
All are invited to learn to sing
I am who am's song

'Tis the walk without legs
I am who am walks
In each and every one of me
I am who am

I am who am is hidden treasure
Desiring to make I am who am known
I am who am is the miracle
Being made known

Be!
The footprint of a miracle
Upon which the light of life
Has shown
Be!

The footprint of a miracle
Allow the light of light to shine bright
Allow I am who am's presence
Be made known

Breathe in
Breathe out
The breath of life
It is in this breath
I am who am's presence is made known

I am who am is
The presence made known
I am who am is
The light in which
I am who am's presence
Is made known

I am who am
Is oneness
Is I am's presence
Is I am who am
Is I am who am makes known

Remove all the veils
That block the view of ultimate reality
Of life as it is
Of life as it is meant to be

Remove all the veils
That do not allow
One to see me
I am who am

See me
See me alone
In every one
In everything one sees
I am who am
Is the ultimate reality

Breathe in
Breathe out
With every breath
This ultimate reality

Acknowledging, knowing, being
The oneness of one
Is to acknowledge
To know
To be
The ultimate reality of existence
The ultimate reality of me
I am who am

Delight in I am who am's presence
As I am who am delights in the oneness of thee

Jesus was expressing ultimate reality
When he spoke of the reality of oneness
The Father and I are one
Is the ultimate reality

Oneness
Is one in love
Is the ultimate reality
Which frees

If one would walk the path of oneness
One would be walking on the path of ultimate reality
Oneness is one
In love
Is
Now be

Once one has been baptised
In the fan of I am who am's love
I am who am is free
To walk freely
In such a vessel of love
I am who am walks free

Freedom is to be found in the present moment
Freedom is to be found in me
In the timelessness of the timeless one
I am who am is the present moment
Which frees

There is no past
No future
In the present moment of me
I am who am
Walk freely

No future
In the present moment of me
I am who am
Walk freely

A 'yes' given in the present moment
Is the 'yes' of lovers
'Yes maybe tomorrow'
Is the 'yes' of those
On the road of intent

Give one's yes in the present moment
And the walk begins
I am who am
Is the walk
Always begins

Being faithful to the path given
Is being faithful to oneness
Is I am who am being faithful to ultimate reality
Is I am who am being faithful unto the oneness
Of one of I am who am's
Ultimate reality

In the mystery of oneness
Is one
How else could it be
I am who am is
The mystery on oneness
Is one in love
Is ultimate reality

Touching the oneness
Is touching me
I am who am touching the oneness
Is me touching me
It is in the oneness
One touches true reality

When I am who am
Looks in a thousand mirrors
I am who I am sees one thousand reflections
Of me
I am who I am
One only has to look and see

All are invited
Although in this conference of the birds
Most are ignorant, fearful
Or rationalise away the oneness
Of I am who I am's presence
Close their eyes
To the Goddess of love
As they walk on their ways

The invitation to say, 'yes'
Is extended to all of me

The freedom to say, 'yes'
To say, 'no'
To say, 'not yet'
To say, 'get thee away from me'
Is the freedom given
To those in human form

Such freedom has not been given
To those in the higher and lower realms of nature

Each is faithful to
The nature given to thee

A leaf is faithful to
The nature of a leaf
No, 'yes' or, 'no' is asked for
Or given

For the Angels of the spiritual realm
Their freedom is always, 'yes'
For they, freed of the flesh
Freed of the veils
Can truly see

For those who can see
For those who have said, 'yes'
For those who have surrendered to the ultimate truth
The ultimate reality
The yes is always given

For they are fully an expression
A reflection
Of me
I am who I am

In them in oneness
I am who am can only see
I am who I am
Me
Fully, freely

'Tis why I am who I am can say
See me
See me alone
In every one
In everything one sees

In the mirror of the heart
One can only see oneness
The oneness in all
Its expressions
The oneness of me
I am who I am

When one views reality as it is
When one sees reality as it
Is meant to be
One sees this world
This existence
This realm
With the eyes of the heart
With the eyes and ears of me
I am who am
Look, listen, see

As water poured into water
As light shined upon light
Such is the oneness in
I am who am's sight

One dwells in a reality
Where it appears darkness overwhelms light
One dwells in a reality
Where one cries out in the middle of the night

But blood can be turned into milk
And greed in to compassion
As the Buddhist prophet did say
Darkness is only a shadow of the light

The darkness can be absorbed away
As the four noble truths which Buddha heard (1)
In the silence
Did say

Light can overcome darkness
Just as generosity overcomes greed

But the human must say 'yes'
It desires to overcome its ignorance
Of reality
As it is meant to be

The human must say, 'yes'
Beloved
Grant us wisdom
To set ourselves free

I am who am is
The wisdom to set this realm
This reality
Free
Free to be
As it is intended to be

Free to be
A world of lovers
Free to be
Washed in divine love
Free to be an outward expression
Of the oneness of one in love collectively

Many paths have been given
124,000 messengers have been sent
As the Sufis proclaim (2)
What more must be given
To those who say they walk
In the I am who am's name

Lord Buddha
Lord Krishna
Yahweh
Whatever name is spoken
I am who am responds
To that name

Lord Jesus
Prophet Moses
In the name of nothingness, Allah

One only has to step towards God
And one will find her
Running in the direction
Where she heard one's cry

It is at that moment
One feels in real time
The embrace of the Divine

Embraced in the arms of the Divine
One can see this world as it is
One can be about working for the world
As it is meant to be

I am who am is
The world as it is
I am who am is
The world as it is meant to be

Embraced in the light of love
Walk freely
Embraced in a light divine
I am who am
Walks freely
In the vessel which is one's temporary home

Let go of the vessel
Come home
Be home
In me
I am who am
For that is ultimate reality

Be a fragrance of me
I am who am
Wherever one walks
Wherever one roams
In oneness is one
One is always walking home

In oneness is one
In love
I am who am
Is home

Be one in love
Be one in oneness
Be!
Home
Wherever one shall roam

I am who am
Is home
Wherever one shall roam

Be one in me
As oneness is thee
Be!
The oneness of one
Be!

(1) -The 'Four Noble Truths' - contain the essence of the Buddha's teachings. The four principles are:
The truth of suffering (Dukkha).
The truth of the origin of suffering (Samudāya).
The truth of the cessation of suffering (Nirodha).
The truth of the path to the cessation of suffering (Magga).

(2) - Sufis (Sufism) - mystical Islamic belief and practice in which Muslims seek to find the truth of divine love and knowledge through direct personal experience of God.

7. A Feather on the Breath of God

In the oneness of one
In the oneness of the sun

One is one in oneness
When the human and divine kiss
One is one in oneness
When the beloved and the self kiss
One is one in oneness

It is a state, a reality
For which the human is unaware
The beloved offers glimpses and glances
So the human does not despair

It is the glimpse
The glance
That lets the human know
That there is more going on here
Than meets the naked 'I'.
It is the glimmer, the grace
Which makes the human cry

When the human comes to realise
The reality of the divinity within
When the human
Touches the place of no sin

When the human gets a glimpse
Of the ultimate reality
It is at that moment
The human is freed

Free to let go of the feet of clay
Free to be a speck of dust
At the foot of one's master

Free to see a glimpse of life
As it is
Of life of the hereafter

I am who am
Is
A glimpse of the present moment
A glance of the hereafter

I am who am
Is
The now
Is
The hereafter
Follow I am's footsteps
Into the hereafter

The miracle of oneness
The miracle of now
All comes to life
In the here and now

This love is real
This love is alive
This love is a gift
This love tells thee why

Why one exists
Why one came
Into being

It has never been about thee
No matter how hard the ego
Strives to survive

It is and has only been about a oneness
A oneness in which the human gets lost
A oneness deep inside
To be lost in the company
Of those Lost in God
Is what the path is about
This journey one has been on

This walk of the forever
Is a walk of oneness in one
This walk of the forever
Is a walk in the sun

Recognise this ray of light
This spark of the divine
The light
The love
Which makes one, one
It is the spark of his light of love
Which makes one, one

I am who am is a hidden treasure
Desiring to make
I am who am's self known
It is within created space
I am who am's face is made known

See I am who am
In every face one sees
See I am who am
In every leaf
In every tree

I am who am is
The reality of thee
Come see I am who am's face
Free
Freely

In the mystery of forever
In the miracle of now
I am who am's presence
Is embodied in every now

Come sit, walk, dwell
In I am who am's presence
I am who am
Will show you how

To be lost in God
Is to be lost in me
I am who am
Come now and be lost
In the presence of me
I am who am frees

The journey continues
The walk moves on
I am who am washes off the dust
That clings to one's feet
I am who am bathes one
In love complete

It takes a long time to be pregnant in God
But once the birth has taken place
The moving finger writes
And having writ moves on

One's moving fingers
Have been set free
They have written the word
Given unto them

No more can be asked
In the heart of the friend
I am who am is the heart
Of the friend
As Jesus said
I call you my friends

To be servant of the one
Is to be servant of all
Listen deep in the silence
And one will know I am who am's call
To be faithful in oneness
Is to surrender to I am who am's call

For in the mystery
In the miracle of oneness
One surrenders one's 'separateness'
In the one and all

Surrender one's earthly identity
In the one and all
In oneness one is made free to wander
As I am who am wills

In oneness
One is a feather on the breath of God
In oneness there is no distinction
Between love, lover and the beloved

Love is what oneness is based upon
Love is the lyrics of the beloved's song
Love is the verse, the stanza
Love is in every note

Love is the music of the heart
Sing I am who am's song
For it is only love
I am who am imparts

Love is the answer
To every question
Found in the human heart

I am who am is the question
Is
The answer
In every human heart

I am who am pervades all creation
Created out of love
It is love which perfuses every cell
Of every being
Formed out of formlessness
With a love
Only I am who am can impart

Keep listening deep for the meaning of these days
Keep listening for the message being imprinted on the heart
Keep listening deep for it is only
Love which I am who am imparts
Love is being played out in the chakra of the heart (1)

One has been listening to the eulogy to be spoken
When one leaves one's earthly ways
Just a simple expression of love
As one walks on into one's always

Walk on
Walk on now
Into one's always

In the mystery of one
In the miracle of oneness
Thou art but a footprint
Of a miracle
As one walks into the always

In oneness
One knows the suffering
And tries to heal it
In oneness one sees the wrong
And tries to right it

In oneness one is pained by war
And tries to stop it
It is oneness which allows one to see
Reality as it is
Reality
As it is meant to be
I am who am is reality as it is meant to be

Listen deep
Listen deep to me
I am who am in the depths of thee
I am who am

The meaning of oneness
The meaning of one
Is deeper than the word written

Let go of the words
Touch only the depths
Of the oneness of one
Be touched by the oneness
As one is touched
By the rays of the sun

Be touched in I am who am's love
Like butterfly wings upon the heart
Be touched in I am who am's love
For it is love, only love
Which I am who am imparts
I am who am is
The love found in every human heart

Love me
Love me alone
In the heart of every thee
Love me love me alone
In I am who am's freedom
Be free

I am who am's freedom
Is the freedom which frees
In the miracle of the oneness
Of one
Love freely

In freedom speak the word
One is given to say
In freedom speak as one walks
In one's always

A word is given sometimes
To confront and confound
A word is given sometimes to console and show respect
One need only be faithful to the word given

Like Khidr speak only (2)
What one is given to say
Be Khidr on one's way
Be faithful
To the path given

Be!
On ones way
Be on ones way
This day
Be!

(1) - Chakra (Sanskrit) - is a centre of energy in the body.
(2) - Khidr or al-Khidr (The Green One) - is a mystical figure that some believe to be described in the Koran as a righteous servant of God, possessing a great wisdom or mystic knowledge. He is often seen as a messenger pointing those who seek, towards God.

8. Listen with the Heart

Be!
The presence of I am who am
To everyone one meets
Just as I am who am is in every one, one meets

The mirror of the heart reflects only one
Me
I am who am

When I am who am looks into one thousand hearts
I am who am sees one thousand faces of me
I am who am
All with different facial features
All faces of I am who am

See me
See me alone
Is not empty rhetoric
It is the reality

I am who am is a hidden treasure
I am who am is making I am who am known
See me
See me alone
In every reality one is shown

Look deeply
Listen with the heart

When the mind is hammered
In to the heart
It is I am who am's truth
Which I am who am imparts

I am who am is
In the depth of heart
Come sit, walk, dwell
In I am who am's heart

In the heart of oneness
In the heart of one
I am who am is
There is only one

Touch the mystery
Know the mystery of oneness
Know the mystery of one's self

I am who am is
A hidden treasure
Revealing (to) I am who am to
I am
Who am
Self

I am who am is mirror, beauty, eye
I am who am is love, lover, beloved
I am who am is here
Now, this why

I am who am lies hidden
In every part of creation
The human eye can see
By only opening the inner eye can one see
I am who am is the inner eye

Now look
Now see
Only me
In the mystery of oneness

Is one
Only me
I am who am

All is a living entity of me
I am who am
Come know this reality
Freely
Come and see me
Freely
Come
And see

In the mystery of forever
In the mystery of now
There is no time
To/in oneness
All is only now
Be!
Now

For that is all there is
Now
Only now
Be!
Now

In the mystery of one
In the mystery of love
There is only now
Be one
Be love
Be now
Be!

The true beauty is
Not one's humanity
It is but a temporary state in a space
Where one day is like a thousand

The human reality
Is but a speck of dust
In the windstorms
Of divine reality

Be faithful to the speck of dust
For it is an expression
Of the reality of me
I am who am

Oneness is freeing
Surrendering to the oneness
Is being one
In which one is

Words cannot describe what is
I am who am is
What is
Be!

Don't be fooled by the bark of the tree
The outer coverings are not the essence of me
The outer covering is thrown into the fire
And burned once its purpose has been fulfilled

When no more can be asked
When no more can be given
Oneness returns to the ocean of love
Oneness returns to oneness

A oneness one never left
A oneness to which one never returns

For in the mystery of oneness
Is one
There is no beginning
There is no end
There is only now
Be!

Oneness is one
In love
In me
I am who am
Be!
Be!

9. The Landmines of the Heart

In the silence of me
In the silence which frees
Be free
In me
Be! Free
Be! One
In me

I am he whom I love
He whom I love
Is me
Be free
Be me

Oneness in one only frees
Free to see reality as it is
Free to be reality as it is
I am who am is

In the mystery of oneness
In the mystery of now
I am who am shows one
How to live
How to be
In this dream of reality

Be faithful to the present moment
Knowing that it will float away
Be faithful to the present moment
For that is all that is given to man to play

The present moment is the now
I am who am dwells in each day
Be one in oneness
Be one in the gods and goddesses at play

One worries about the suffering
Suffering is part of the fabric
Of this existence
Suffering is a way of life

Suffering can be overcome
Seek out its causes
As Lord Buddha has taught,
'Demine all the landmines of the heart'

Greed, hatred and ignorance
Has overwhelmed the land
All these can be demined
If people would give a damn
To stop this suffering
In the land

I am who am
Is
The path
Is
The way
To overcome suffering
To keep the suffering at bay

Many messengers have been sent
124,000 by the Sufi claim
I am who am has sent many more
People who in the silence
Come with no name

To the Sufis, Khidr is the name
I am who am roams this creation
In the people of no name
Khidr is their nickname

I am who am sees the suffering
With the eyes of such as these
I am who am touches the suffering
With the hands of these

I am who am sees the suffering
Which free-will has done
I am who am sees
I am who am sees
I am who am ultimately frees
I am who am frees

The world has been given many examples
Of those who walk in I am who am's ways
Many a Khidr
Wanders on the earth's pathways

Many a Khidr has glanced upon
With eyes of love
For it is I am who am glancing
Upon with eyes of love

Whenever there is a moment of mercy
Whenever one is glanced upon with compassionate eyes
Whenever one offers a weary walker a ride
It is I am who am walking
It is I am who am offering a ride

For in the mystery of oneness is one
How else could it be?
I am who am is the mystery of oneness
Is one

To dwell in oneness
To dwell in me
Is to be
Seen and unseen
Clean and unclean
Loved and unloved
Free and unfree
I am who am is one in all
How else could it be

Who am I not
As the Sufi sage did reply
In oneness is one
I am who am is one
I am who am dwells in all
In all I am who am resides

See me
See me alone
Is not a nice mantra to repeat and repeat
See me alone
See me alone
Are words to reflect the reality
Words to set one free
To see reality as it is
Reality as it is meant to be seen

I am who am is reality
Reality as it is reality
As it is meant to be seen

See me
See me alone
In all of creation

See with the eyes of the heart
See with the inner eye
For it is I am who am
It is I

For it is and has only been about love
Since the beginning of created time
Why else live and breathe
Or have a being
If not for love

'Tis the only reason to open one's eyes in the morning
The only reason to close one's eyes at night
See with the eyes of love
See with the inner eye

Hammering one's mind into the heart
Is to see the world
With the eyes of love
To see the world with the eye
Of me
I am who am
The one who sees

Seeing the world with the inner eye
Is to see like me
I am who am
See
Be
Me
I am who am
Be

10. True Healing is Within

Be silent in the silence
In me
I am who am

It is in the silence
One can see
One can hear
One can touch the truth of me
I am who am

In silence
I am who am walks freely
Come see
Hear, touch, walk freely

In silence
One must learn to crawl
Before one can walk
In silence
One can learn to walk
I am who am's walk
To speak I am who am's talk

It is in the silence
The dead fish come alive (1)
The blind one sees
The deaf one hears
I am who am sets free

Jesus worked miracles
When he walked upon the land
The outward act was to teach
Of the interior reality

Like Maha his outward words (2)
Were trying to reflect the interior realities

Maha spoke of landmines
Saying the mother of all the landmines
In the ground
Are the landmines in the heart
'Tis these inner landmines
Which need to be demined
Before peace can even begin
To get a start

The healing of the flesh
Was only an outward expression of the
Inner realities
The true healing is within
The true healing which frees
I am who am
Oneness in one truly frees

If all is a spark of me
If all bear a divine reality
How else could it be
I am who am
Free
Be!

Be the freedom which frees
Be! The love which loves

Know/Be
The ultimate reality of me in me
I am who am
Know the love
Be

Free
Simple loving freely
Be!

There are aspects of me
I am who am
Which I am who am discloses freely
There are other aspects
Which one must sit in silence
Patiently

For these are slowly to be revealed
Slowly disclosed
For one to see, to be
To reveal all at once
Would overwhelm the human vessel
Would be too much for
Unprepared humanity

I am who am
Prepares one's humanity
To see one's divinity

I am who am bakes and boils
Cooks like peas in a pot
Cooks until one is well done
I am who am burns, burns one
In the Fana of love (3)

When I am who am reveals oneself
All floss and jetsam
Must be burned away
Along with all concepts of me
I am who am

Then I am who am reveals
I am who am's self
As me
I am who am

I am who am frees one
To walk without a shadow
To sing without an echo
To love without leaving a trace
I am who am frees
With I am who am's grace

I am who am is freedom
Walking in place
To see the face of God
In every face is
I am who am's grace

See with the eye of the inner heart
See I am who am's face in every one, one meets
See with the eye of inner reality
See with the eye which allows one to see freely

See me
See me alone
That is
The look
Which frees
See me
Be me
Freely

The father and I are one
Are words Jesus used
To express his earthly reality

He described his earthly existence
In terms of the divine reality
That is how Jesus was free

When one fully understands
Fully comprehends
Ones earthly reality
One is free
To free others
To be free

One frees
As Jesus frees
One sees
As Jesus sees

This is true of all true
Messengers of me
I am who am

Be!
A true messenger of me
I am who am
Free

In silence one experiences
The freedom which is to be expressed
In the outer realms

Silence is freedom
Before the word takes flesh
Limiting itself
Freely to the human realities

Silence is always within
'Tis the solitude in the crowd
'Tis in silence one dwells
Before the word is spoke out loud

I am who am is the silence before
The word is spoken out loud

'Tis why one is always invited
To sit within me
I am who am is the silence
Which frees

Free to be the truth
Free to live it freely
Free to always walk
In the silence
Of me
I am who am
Free to walk freely
In me
I am who am

This human existence is all about freedom and freeing
Freed
One's self is free to help set others free

Free to see reality as it is
Free to see reality as it is meant to be seen
Free to be reality as it is meant to be

I am frees
I am frees
I am free

Free the crippled spirits
Even as Jesus freed the crippled flesh
The outer expression
Of an inner happiness

What is easier to say
Thy sins are forgiven
Or pick up thy mat and walk

Jesus always spoke to the inner reality
As did Lord Buddha, Lord Krishna
The prophets, Moses and Mohammed, Mary

All who speak freely in me
Listen for the truth in those
Who speak freely

For their words come out of the silence
Come from the heart of me
I am who am

This is the heart to heart transmission
One has heard spoken of
This is the heart to heart transmission
Spoken with words of love

I am who am
Is
The silence which loves silently
Love within I am who am's love
Love silently

Love the silence
One comes out of
Love the silence

To which one shall return
Silence begets silence
Love begets love

Water poured into water
Drown in me
I am who am

Love freedom
Love freely
I am who am loves freedom
I am who am loves freely
Love
Love like me
A freeing love
A loving freedom
Free

I am loves
I am who am loves freely

Once all the words have been written
Spoken
Be silence
Rest in me
I am who am
Silently

Come into the silence of this day
Come now
Come always into the silence
Silently
I am who am is silence, silently

Be silence
Be silent
In me
I am who am
Be!

(1) - Gospel of Thomas - Apocryphal story.
(2) - Maha - Maha Ghosananda.
(3) - Fana - Sufi term that means to die before one dies. Literally passing away or annihilation of the self.

11. The Silence of the Friend

Be silent
In the silence

Be silent in the friend
I am who am is silence
I am who am is friend

Go beyond the silence
Go deeper
And deeper
Into the friend

I am who am
Is silence beyond silence
I am who am
Is the silence of the friend

I am who am calls each friend
Know the silence
Know the friend
Know the oneness
Know love
Without end

I am who am
Is
Silent love
Without end
Be!
The silence of the friend

Beyond the beyond
Beyond the oneness
Beyond the friend
Beyond the nothingness
Without end

Beyond what is beyond
Whatever will be
Beyond any concept of life
Any concept of eternity

Beyond the freedom which frees
Beyond the seen and unseen
Beyond the light
Beyond the darkness of me

Beyond any glance of ultimate truth
Beyond any glance of ultimate reality
Beyond the beyond
Of me as me
Beyond all knowns and unknowns

Beyond inescapable realities
Beyond any clue of I am who am is
I am who am is
I am who am is freely

Blessed are the eyes of the heart
Which simply see me
I am who am
When I am who am
Opens the eyes of the heart
One sees freely

When I am who am
Touches the heart
The deaf hear
The mute speak
The blind see
The slave is freed

I am who am
Touches the heart
Of every one of thee
In oneness
Is one
In love
In me
I am who am

I am who am carries one
Into a deeper silence in every chamber
Of the heart
Of me

Written words
Human concepts
Of the reality
Of the ultimate truth
The ultimate reality of me
I am who am

Come silently into the presence
Of silence
Silence comes silently
Be bathed in the light of silence
Silently

I am who am is the light of silence
Which baths all in silence
Silently

Be lit with the light of silence
Silently

Let silence light the path one walks upon
Let silence sing I am who am's song
In silence one never gets it wrong

In silence
It is
I am who am singing
I am who am's song

Singing without an echo
Singing without a song
Singing without a note
Singing with one's clay feet still on the ground
Singing without making a sound

When I am who am sings
There is no sound

A song sung is like a spinning top
It turns, turns
And never stops

Be a whirling dervish (1)
Sing I am who am's song
In the silence which never stops

A never ending silence
Sung in every human heart
I am who am is the
Never ending silence
Sung in every heart

For in the silence
There is no echo
In silence there is no shadow
Within silence one leaves no trace
Silence is what silence is,
Grace

Far beyond all one knows
Far beyond all one will ever conceive
I am who am is
I am who am frees
Inconceivably free
Unbelievably made known

This is the light which shines beyond
Beyond known and unknown
This is the light which glows
Upon the known and unknown

One belongs to a tradition
Which allows one to see
Reality as it is
Reality as it is meant to be
I am who am is reality
As it is meant to be

Now Be!

Those of us who loved him
And bring him to his rest today
Pray that what he meant to us
And did for others will
One day come to pass for the whole world
Are words of eulogy

The spiritual aspirant is dead
Come
Walk home freely
I am who am
Walks thee home freely

I am who am's reflection
Falls freely upon the mirror of the heart
In silent reflection

I am who am
In love imparts
A silent word
A silent reflection
Upon a silent heart
I am who am is
Be!

(1) – Dervish - Member of the Sufi order who has taken vows of poverty and austerity.

12. The Divinity Within

God of Silence
Goddess of oneness
God of one

Spirit of light
Spirit of love
Spirit of one

One in oneness
One in light
One in love

I am who am
Is
One
In light
And love
I am who am is

One is awashed in silence
One is bathed in it

Silence is the breath one breathes
Silence is the water one drinks
Silence is

Be at home in me
Be at home in it
I am who am is
Oneness is
Be!

In the mystery of oneness
In the mystery of silence
Oneness is one in silence

Oneness is one in me
Expresses
The same reality

Be one
In silence
Be one in me
Be one in oneness
Be!

Freedom is a gift of silence
Freedom is a gift in me
I am who am

One who walks in silence
Day in day out
Is free
One always dwells in silence
That is the reality

One always walks in freedom
Move freely in the silence
I am who am
Free

I am who am
Is freeing
I am who am
Frees

Be! Free
Be! Freeing
Be! Me

Touch one's divinity
Which lies within one's humanity
That is the reality
Which frees

Aware of acknowledging
The spark of divinity within
Is the reality which frees
Free to see this existence
As it is
Free to see this existence
As it is meant to be

Free to walk freely
In the reality of one's divinity

Nothing to fear when one sees this world
With the eyes of the reality
Of the divinity
Me
Me within a vessel of clay

I am who am
Walking within
When all else walks away

Realise the divine essence
Within this vessel of clay
Recognise the reality of me
I am who am
Walking with feet of clay

Nothing to fear
When one walks in reality
Nothing to make one proud
Or the reality is not you

This is the reality of oneness
This is oneness
Is one
In love

Freeing love
Loving freedom
Freeing reality

I am who am invites
I am who am brings one home
Home within the heart of oneness
Home within a love that frees
I am who am
Is a love which frees

A freeing love which allowed al-Hallaj to say (1)
I am God
Before he was cut and quartered
And carried away

A freeing love which carried Jesus to His Calvary
It is such freeing love which frees one to speak the truth
To see
With the eye of the heart

To see as I am who am sees
I am who am sees
With freeing love
I am who am sees freely

Free his world with eyes of love
From all which leaves it so un-free
See me
Free me
In all one sees
Free freely

Love without leaving a trace
Be a fragrance
Of I am who am's grace
Let it be quietly known
I am who am walks in this place

Be faithful to the truth
Of the reality one sees
One sees with the eyes of oneness
One sees with the eyes of me
I am who am

Be seeing
Be seen
As me
I am who am
See
Believe
Be!

Be a creative force of being
For I am who am is love
For I am who am is love
Be a redemptive force of love
For I am who am is redeeming

Oneness is one in love
Is a force
Is a power
Which is redeeming

If you can turn this world as it is
Into the reality it is meant to be
Love is a power
A force that frees freely

Love with a love
Which loves freely
I am who am is
Love
Love freely
Be!
I am who am
Be!

(1) - Mansur al-Hallaj - was a mystic and a revolutionary writer and teacher of Sufism.

13. A Flash in the Realm of No Time

Silence dwells in silence
Silence sits in silence
Silence is the silence
Of me
I am who am

One is engulfed in silence
Silence permeates one's being
Silence flows through one's veins
Silence is the source of silence
Silence is a goddess of no names

Out of and within the silence
One came
Into being
Back to and within the silence
One shall return
And always remain

This life
This existence has been a flash
In the realm of no time

Be faithful to the flash
I am who am
Is a god/dess of no name

Each drop in the ocean of love
Each drop in the sea of humanity
Is the essence of the one who frees
I am who am
Is
The one who frees

Being is
To be
Free
In me
I am who am

The physical world is limited
The spirit is free
The spirit walks freely
In I am who am
In me

Walk on freely
In me
I am who am

In oneness one walks
Wherever I am who am walks
In this reality
Forever in a world of no time
One walks in me
I am who am

Not a play on words
'Tis a play on oneness

Oneness holds a pen
With hands of dust
And water and clay
Oneness rises up in the morning
With feet of clay

Oneness lies as dust at the foot of its master
For oneness is the master
Oneness is the feet of clay
Oneness is
What oneness is

Walk with these feet of clay
Until dust they shall return
Then one walks on
One does not walk away
No more than Maha or Fujii have walked away (1)

They dwell in the hearts
They dwell in the feet
Of those who walk in their ways
The spirit walks on
No longer limited by feet of clay

The spirit which is at home
In silence
Silence is the spirit's home

It is within the silence
One is already
One is always
Home

In silence one is home
Even while still bearing feet of flesh
In the silence
One comes home
One comes to know
Full and complete happiness

'Tis why I am who am
Has always in no time
Invited all into the silence
Of no time and no place
One is already and always home
Within I am who am's grace

Thrust into the silence
Even as one is engulfed in it
Silence is the home of the atheist and mystic
Labels established by man
What does love got to do with it

Love speaks with words of love
Silence speaks in silence
One dwells in silent love
One sits in loving silence

One in love
One in silence
Oneness is one
In love

The word comes out of the silence
The word takes on flesh
In love

Silent love
Frees the word to speak
In loving silence
The word is released

If spoken in love
The word returns to the silence
As the dove returned to Noah's ark

Thrown into the abyss
It is love
Only love
I am who am imparts

Free will is given
To love or not love
To fly into the storm
Or return to the ark
Mission accomplished
Until the next mission departs

'Tis a walk of forever
When perceived by the eyes of finite time

The walk is always now
In I am who am's 'time'
Always here
Now this
In I am who am only now exists

In faithfulness
To the present moment
I am who am
Is
Love
Is
Silence
Is
Oneness
Is

Oneness
Is one
In silent love
Be!
For I am who am is
Be!
For I am who am is

(1) - Fujii - A Japanese Buddhist monk who founded an Order devoted to eradicating war and nuclear armaments. Maha refers to Maha Ghosananda, a Cambodian monk who led peace walks.

14. The Ultimate Reality

In the oneness of me
In the oneness of thee
I am who am frees

Oneness without distinction
Oneness is one
Just as all walk under one sun
One does perceive the sun in the sky
It is visible to the naked eye

The oneness is unseen to the naked eye
Open the eye of the heart
Learn how to fly

Nothing can break the transmission of me
I am who am
It is
I am who am writes
It is I am who am sets free
The human is invited to touch
The wonder of me

I am who am
Is a hidden treasure
Desiring to make myself made known
In the night's sky a light has shone
Make it known
Make it known
Make this light known

One has been given many teachers
Many guides
Now is the time to share the teachings
That are held
That have been disclosed inside

One can only write what one hears
Because of those who taught one how to listen
How to listen deep inside
I am who am speaks from deep inside

Write what one hears
Don't be afraid
Don't be shy
Transmissions have been given
Since the beginning of human time

I am who am does not hide deep inside
I am who am is present
To all who open the eye and see
I am who am opens the eye
Come look, listen see and believe
Be a witness
To all the inner eye
Has been given to see

The journey into oneness
Is no journey at all
It is the acknowledgement
Of the reality of it all
It is in oneness
One is love

There is no masking
No veils
No obstacles
To see
The world as it is
The world as it is meant to be

I am who am
Is the world
As it is
I am who am
Is the world
As it is meant to be

See me
See only me
In every reality one sees
For in the oneness of one
How else could it be
Be witness of
Be witness to be
I am who am
Be!

Be human as one recognises one's divinity
A spark of light
A spark of love
The loving light of divinity

However inadequate the words may be
Know the love
Know the light
Be!
The spark of divinity which only frees

For those who have the light in the eye
For those who have the eye to see
They can never deny the deeper realities

Be!
The light which frees others to see
Listen to those who have the eyes to see
Free as they free
Free others freely

Use whatever words
Use whatever language of the heart that frees
Speak to the heart
Open the inner eye
So the blind may see

See the inner
See the ultimate reality
Of what this existence is about
Of how this existence is meant to be
I am who am frees all
To see

When all the veils have been removed
One is fully free
I am who am sees freely
With the eyes of me in thee
For in the mystery of oneness in one
How else could it be

Oneness is one
In love
Oneness frees
Oneness is me
I am who am
Be!

The miracle of oneness
Is how Jesus helped the blind to see
The deaf hear
The lame walk freely

He opened the inner eye of the heart
He freed people freely
In the oneness of one
In love
He walked freely
He freed others freely

Not limited by human expectations
Of what divinity is
Not limited by the veils
Of his time and place

He freed for he knew
Reality how it is
He freed for he knew
Reality as it is meant to be
He freed freely
For he had the eye to see

The same be true for all
The spiritual masters
Who take the time to see
Listen in the dark dazzling silence
Of love
And
Be!

There are no limitations
In I am who am
Who am me
Be! Free
Know one's humanity
Know the divinity of me
I am who am

To know oneself
Is to know one's lord
It has been said
To know oneself is to acknowledge me
I am who am
Walking in feet of clay

Be faithful to those feet in this realm
In other realms one is invited
Be faithful in other ways
Be faithful to the path given
Be faithful to the feet of clay

When all the veils are lifted
One is invited to walk in other ways
I am who am is the way
Keep listening
Deep in the silence of love
And know the way

Be free in I am who am
For I am who am frees
I am who am frees the way

No word need be spoken
No song need be sung
For the beloved, lover and love

Walk as one
No word need be spoken
In the oneness of love

Enlightenment is not given
Heaven and hell need not be feared
Or yearned for
I am who am
Is here now
This I am who am
Is the oneness of one
Be!
One in the oneness of one
One love
One lover
One beloved
One!

Be free in such oneness
Be free in one
I am who am is free
I am who am is there
In one
Love
Lover
Beloved
One!

Sit is the silence
Walk in the sun
Know!
Be only love
I am who am
Love

15. I Am Who Am is

The bond with the beloved
Is the only bond to speak of
It is the only bond of love

All other bonds are variations
On the theme
Variations of the primordial covenant

I am who am
Revealing I am who am's self
Unto me
I am who am
The ultimate reality

Love is the answer
To every question of the heart
Love is the ultimate

What is love
It is the ultimate question
I am who am
Places in the human heart
Come into the silence
To know the answer to this question
Which I am who am imparts

It is the only question one needs to know
One needs to answer
On this journey called life

I am who am
Is
The question
I am who am
Is
The answer
I am who am is the ultimate reality

All which lives and breathes
Is an expression of this reality
There are many leaves, many branches, many trees
Each an aspect of what is called nature

Love is part of what is called divine nature
It is the root, trunk, branches
Leaves of every human tree
Love is the ultimate nature
Love is the ultimate harmony

Love is the axis this world
This existence is spun upon
Love is the instrument, the music
The notes in which the sounds of love
Are heard and perceived

I am who am is love
In the ultimate ultimately

Searching for love in all the wrong places
Is a misnomer
For love can be discovered
Love can be expressed
In every aspect of the human reality

Blessed are those who have eyes to see
And believe every aspect of
I am who am
Me

Be lost in love
Be lost in the company
In the companions of those lost in God

Love is the only reason to walk
Live
Breathe

Breathe in
Breathe out
The ultimate reality of me
I am who am
Me

Inviting others into the silence
Is inviting others
To come, to know, to touch, to realise
The ultimate reality of their existence
The very reality of me
I am who am

I am who am is a hidden treasure
Waiting to be found
Waiting to reveal I am who am's presence
In the silence of me
I am who am
I am who am sits in the silence of ultimate truth
Ultimate reality

Silence fills empty spaces
Silence fills empty rooms
That is the invitation to empty oneself
Of all one is
All one knows
So as to know

Be made known in the silence of me
Only me
Only love
Only ultimate truth
Only ultimate reality

Empty oneself of all concepts, thoughts, visions
Of who I am who am
So I am who am can be
Fully present
Fully me
I am who am

The human in its humanity
Can never grasp the length
And width
And depth of love

The human can only get glimpses
Glances
A whiff
Of me

So empty yourself of every thought
Idea, concept of me
I am who I am
So I am who am
May be fully present
In ultimate reality

Reduce oneself to zero
And know only me
Let go of all the mental constructs
Perceptions, interpretations of me

Don't limit I am who am with human limitations
Be totally lost
In I am who am
As
I am who am is totally free
In human reality

Let go of all human limitations
In the humans' understanding of me
I am who am
Ultimately

Don't throw around words in silence
Be silent in silence
Be silent in the presence of silence
Be silent in the silence of ultimate reality

It is the place
The space
The realm
The existence
The wordless wordy description
Of me
I am who am

I am who am
Is
Be!
The Is

For it is
I am who am
Be!
Is!

For I am who am
Is

16. Faithful to the Face Given

There is nothing but nothingness
One is completely lost in me
I am who am

There is no I, we, you, them
In I am who am
There is only me
I am who am

To be lost in the company
Of those lost in God
Is to be lost in me
I am who am

To be lost
To non-exist
What is the mystery
One tries to define, to understand in human terms
Which belongs to divine mystery

One gets lost in places one does not know
One is lost in the unknown
One is lost in the unknowable
Come, be lost in me
Freely

Once one gives one's yes
One becomes lost consciously, knowingly
Giving one's yes freely
One jumps into the ocean of love
Freely
Nakedly

It is in drowning in the ocean of love
One is freed, freely
Drown
Be lost in me

I am who am takes one there
I am who am brings one back
I am who am is just as
I am who am isn't

To be lost in the present moment
Is to be lost in me
I am who am
Be lost
Freely
Consciously
Listen deeply
In the mystery
Listen deeply
In me
I am who am
Be!

Be Freely
Be consciously
Be!

Do not be afraid to be lost in me
Consciously
This has never been
About thee
Knowing the ultimate reality is freeing
Be free

This is what I am who am offers
This is what I am who am discovers
The freedom to be free freely
I am who am frees the human to see

See the reality as it is
See reality as it is meant to be
See
Freely

I am who am is reality as it is
I am who am is reality as it is meant to be
See
Be
I am who am freely
There is no other but me

Know the nothingness
Know Allah (1)
Know me
I am who am

Know me
I am who am in every face one sees
Know the one who looks into the mirror of the heart
And sees only me
I am who am

That is the God consciousness
Of which I am who am speaks
I am who am seeks

See the face of God in every one
One sees
See the face of me

I am who am
See
Only see
Be
Only be

Be faithful to the face
Given to one
In this time and place
Then let it go
Let it be

Listen deeply in the heart of me
I am who am
Listen freely
Listen in me
Listen, see, believe
Be!

(1) - Allah (Arabic) - The God, the deity.

17. The Freedom of All Veils Removed

There is an emptiness in silence
Just as there is a silence in emptiness
It is the sound before the sound
It is the sound of the presence
Of me
I am who am

Listen in
Listen to
This silence
Which engulfs one's very soul

I am who am's presence
Is silence
Know the silence
Know thy soul

Oneness is one
Is formed
Is shaped
In silence
The silence before there was silence
The silence before there was soul

I am who am is the silence
Before the word is formed

Silence is the place where the two seas meet
Bless the Lord
Oh my soul

Silence one was born out of as one was born into
Silence one returns to when the body
The flesh
The word
Returns to whence it came

I am who am is the silence
I am who am is the god
The goddess of no name

Walk in this silence
Silently
Without fear
Without shame
In silence know I am who am's name
A silent bow to the goddess of no name

To be conscious of the silence
To be conscious of me
I am who am
Is to begin to know ultimate truth
Ultimate reality
Is to begin to know the ultimate me
I am who am
Be
Free

Free in oneself
Free in the self
Be free of the self and non-self of thee
Free of the ego
The emotion
The body
The mind
Be free in the oneness of love
Be free

Not empty rhetoric
Ultimate reality
The freedom of all veils removed

Freedom to walk in the midnight sun
Freedom to be free with the free
I am who am is freedom
I am who am frees
Free. Be
Free
Ultimately
Be
Me

Such is the mystery on oneness in one in love

The sacred secret
The sacred mystery
The sacred me
I am who am
Be aware of the ego
Be free of it

In Fana (1)
The ego is annihilated
There remains the essence of me
I am who am

Truth cleans out the house
Allowing only truth to remain
I am who am
Is
The goddess of no name
In the nothing of nothingness
What is there to name

Allah
The nothing
Is I am who am's name
Nothing to name
Be
A goddess of no name
Be nameless
In I am who am's name
Be!

(1) - Fana - Is the Sufi term for passing away, or annihilation of the self.

18. The Power of the Sun

In the nothingness of nothing
There is nothing left to be
In the nothingness of nothing
One is free of all identity

One is free
To be
Only me
I am who am
Be
Free

In this realm
One feels all the burdens
All the hats to wear

One accepts them readily
In order to help free others
Other faces
Of I am who am
Other faces of me

In this realm one can only be faithful
To one's time and place
Knowing one walks in timelessness
Even as one walks in place

One walks on two paths at the same time
Timelessness and in the present moment of no time
One walks in rhyme
In a world out of rhyme
One walks in love
Veils removed

One sees with the inner eye
The eye which sees beyond all the veils
I am who am is beyond the veils

The human must blind the eyes
In the presence of such pure light
But the beloved sees all
For the beloved is the light

In the presence of such light
All the shadows fade away
Light upon light
Is a sign
Of I am who am's presence
Light upon light
Is the presence
Of the goddesses and gods at play

Light shines on a piece of clay
For dust thou art
And unto dust thou shalt return
Light upon light shines through the dust
As dust floats in the air

Light shines upon light
There is nothing to fear
Light shines upon light
I am who am draws near

Fear not
The light does not blind oneness
For oneness is one in love
The light cannot blind
One made from the sun

This is the light which shines
In each and every one
I am who am
Is
The sun
Do not run
Do not hide from the sun

I am who am's light shine in each and everyone
Under the sun
Shine, shine, shine
Be!
One

The power of oneness
The power of one
Is the power of the sun
Shine with the power of one

19. Nothing but Nothingness

To sit in the silence
Of the one who is one
Is to sit in the silence
Of me
I am who am

I am who am is the silence
Which frees
Sit freely in the silence
Of me
I am who am

I am who am
Is
I am who am
Am
Be!

Oneness is one
In love
In me
Be!
Love
Be!
Me
Be!

I am who am frees
Be freely
Love in me

The miracle of the present moment
The miracle of now
Oneness in love in the present moment
Is the way how

There is no past
No future in the present moment
There is only now
I am who am dwells in the now

Be
One
Be now
Be!
One
Within ultimate reality

The power of one
The light of oneness
I am who am shows one how
Light upon light
I am who am shows one how

Purified by pure love
The Fana of the heart (1)
Until there is nothing left
Nothingness I am who am imparts
I am who am is
The nothingness of the heart

There is nothing but nothingness said
Bhai Sahib (2)
As he departs
Be

Nothing in the heart of hearts
I am who am is
Be
In the heart of hearts

No word need be spoken
In the heart of hearts
Only be
Be

(1) - Fana - Is the Sufi term for passing away, or annihilation of the self.
(2) - Bhai Sahib - Is a Punjab and Sikh title of veneration for a male, 'Sir', or 'brother'.

20. The Mystery which Frees

Truth is
I am who am
Be
Peace is
I am who am
Be

Love is
I am who am
Be
Oneness is
I am who am
Be

Just be
I am who am is
In the mystery of oneness
Just be

Live this mystery
Be this mystery
Love this mystery
Be!

The mystery of oneness
The mystery of now
The mystery of me
I am who am

The mystery which frees
I am who am
Be free
For it is in oneness freedom be
That ain't no mystery
How else could it be

Oneness is one
In love
In silence
In me
I am who am

I am who am
Be
One in oneness
One in love
One in silence
One in mystery

For oneness is the secret
Is the Sihr
Of which the Sufis speak
Oneness in love
Is complete

It is of this I am who am speaks
This is love complete

I am who am washes one's feet
In love
In love complete
No mystery in love complete

I am who am is the dust
I am who am
Washes the dust off one's feet
For that is how it is
In love complete

Be one
Be oneness
In love complete
Love oneness
Love all
With love complete

There is no distinction in love complete
See how Jesus washes the feet
Of those he loved
And those who betrayed him

Even as he could read men's hearts
Love loves
With a love complete
To wash away the dust
To wash away the suffering of another
Is an act of love
An act of love complete

Look at Jesus
Look at Maha (1)
At a water blessing

Maha washed away the suffering of war
With simply water
In love complete
Maha washed with love complete

I am who am
Is love complete

Breathe in breathe out
A love complete
I am who am loves
I am who am is
Love complete
Be!

(1) - Maha - Maha Ghosananda.

21. A Piece of Driftwood

No more words need be spoken
No more songs be sung
I am who am already dwells
In the heart of every single one
Oneness is one in love

I am's is a silent presence
I am is in the air one breathes
Breathe in breathe out this presence
Breathe in breathe out
I am who am

As I am who am breathes
Through this flute of human flesh
One art a flute reed
Whom I am who am makes music
Through with I am who am's breath

One art only an instrument
In the hands of God
One art only a container
Which holds I am who am's breath

I am who am
Is
The container
I am who am is
The breath
Oneness is one
In love
In me
I am who am

Know
Be!
The ultimate truth
The ultimate reality
Be!

Silent love
Silent truth
Silent reality
Be!

I am who am free
In the mystery
Of oneness
Is one
How else could it be

The divine communicates in, to, through its created form
Even as the vessel is ignorant of how it was created
And what it was created for

This is true of all creation
Not only the human form
Yet I am who am
Breathes in breathes out
Every created form visible to the naked eye
Visible in the unseen

I am who am is a living treasure
Making I am who am made known
The light shines in hidden treasures
Being made known

I am who am is making known
Be
Made known
Be
Know
I am who am made known

This realm is a continual drowning
A drowning in the ocean of love
Each wave takes one deeper
'n' deeper in the one
Which is only
Only love

This life realm is a continual drowning
A drowning in the one ocean of love
One must let go
Of all one knows and believes
In the ocean of love

'Cos it's not like that
As the Sufi master says
Continual drowning means
One is in over one's head
In continual drowning one is being led
In continual drowning one is always in
Over one's head.

One is just a piece of driftwood
Blown about by the winds
And currents
Of the sea
Even while bearing the reality of me
Be driftwood
Be me
I am who am

Each is an aspect
A speck of dust
A breath of me
I am who am
Be
Oneness is
One is
The ultimate reality

There is no separation
No distinction
In ultimate truth
Within ultimate reality

All is one
All is free
All is me
I am who am
All is a creation
Of me
I am who am
Be

Be busy upon the path given
Be faithful unto it
For there is a place, a space
For every speck of dust
For I am who am created it

Be one in creation
Be one in me
For it is I am who am
Who has freed
Now
Let it be

22. The Core of One's being

Be one in silence
Be one in love
Remain on the path given
From within
From above

I am who am is
The path given
Within and above
I am who am is love

Love like the one
Who is love
Love each and everyone
Under the sun

I am who am
Is
The sun
The light in the heart
Of each and every one

Love the light seen in each and every one
I am who am sees
I am who am is the light seen
See me

See me alone
In every one, one meets
See me
See me alone
While walking on the street

I am who am
Is
Love me
Love me alone in thee

A separate yet one unity
In the mystery of oneness
In the mystery of one
One learns how to love
Love like the sun

One discovers at the core of one's being
This oneness of one
I am who am
Is love at the core of every living being
I am who am is one

Touch the love
At the core of one's being
Touch me
Only me
I am who am

I am who am is the core of every living being
See me
See me alone
At the core of every living being
I am who am
Is
The core of every living being

Love me
Love me alone
The core of every living being

The light of love lies at the core
Of every living being
Be the light
Be the love
For it is the core of one's being

Be!
What one already is
Be!
I am who am is
Be!
Now Be!

23. Dusting the Mirror of the Heart

In the silence of the present moment
In the silence of me
I am who am

Let a word come forth
Let a word come forth from me
I am who am
Let it be
Let it be

Before a word be spoken
One must be freed
I am who am frees with the love of Fana (1)
With the love of annihilation

The house must be cleansed of all within
Before the truth comes to dwell permanently
Dusting the mirror of the heart
Is part of one's daily reality

One is coming to another curve on the road
I am who am has been giving looks and glances
Leaving hints in your friends
And the people one meets

Listen to the hints
Let a new path unfold

It is I am who am
Who washes one's feet
Within a love complete

I am who am is the path
The walker
The story
Which unfolds
One only to embrace and behold
For this is I am who am's story being told
'Tis a wonder to behold

The words are the same
The depth is too
I am who am
Is what makes you, you

Be! The depth of me
Be! The depth
Which frees one from the limitations
Of one's humanity
For it is just a vehicle, just a vessel
To be one within me
I am who am
Be! One
Be!

The mystery of oneness
Is the mystery of me
I am who am
The mystery of oneness
Is the mystery of me

I am who am is a hidden treasure
Continually making oneness known
'Tis the mystery truth be made known
Oneness is one
In love made known

I am who am
Makes all known
In I am who am
The light has shown
In I am who am
The light glows
Let it glow

Thou art a ray of light
Thou art a drop of rain
Thou art a wonder to behold
Thou are a footprint of a miracle
The miracle of me
I am who am

Why has the human made themselves so un-free?
Entrapped by the landlines of the heart
So un-free
So un-freeing

The human does have a choice
A gift of the nature of the human
To say yes
To say no
To the light within
The eternal light which dwells in mortal human

I am who am is the light which shines
I am who am has laid her heart in thine's
This is the light which shines
The light of I am who am
In thine

In the realm of no separation
Only one light shines
Let is shine
For it will shine through

This is the light of I am who am
This is the light of me
Be!

Be faithful to the light given
Be faithful to me
In oneness is one
No faith is required

For oneness already frees
One to see
Reality as it is
Reality as it is meant to be

For it is the truth which frees
The truth of the reality and unreality
Of this existence
The truth of me
I am who am

Ghandi learned God is truth (2)
It set him free

Sit in the silence
Of the God of truth
Sit in the silence
Of one's always
Sit in the silence of me
I am who am
Be!

(1) - Fana - Is the Sufi term for passing away, or annihilation of the self.
(2) - Mahatma Gandhi - Leader of Indian independence movement.

24. Be! Freely Free

The silence of one is the silence of all
The silence of all is one
Silence is the language all communicate with
In the heart

Silence is the essence of I am who am
In this creation
All created and uncreated forms
Dwell in the silence of me

Sit and listen to/within me
I am who am

A holy sobhet is the communication (1)
I am who am is speaking now
A word of silence spoken
In the silence of now

Before a word is written silence dwells
Before a thought is formulated silence is
Out of Abyss
Of silence
All is come unto the majesty
Of me
I am who am
Come unto the majesty of me
I am who am

Jamal and Jalal (2)
Beauty and Power
Are also part of the essence of me
I am who am
Now Be!

Silence dwells in every breath one breathes
One breathes in
One breathes out constantly
The essence of me
I am who am

When that essence is taken away
Man returns to sand
Man thou art dust
And to dust thou shalt return

One breathes in
One breathes out
The nothingness of me
I am who am

'Tis is the nothingness
All is fully free
Not limited by any of the earthly realities
I am who am's essence is free
I am who am is free
Free Be!

Be freedom
Be free
Be me
In the oneness of I am who am

A divine freedom
Free
Freely
Free
Me
I am who am

Billions of words have been written
Just sit
Just be
In the silence of me
Know the deep and deeper reality
Freely free

This is the reality of all
Who learn how to listen
In the silence of me
I am who am

Silence is sobhet
The conversation of me
I am who am
Speak freely in the silence of me
Silently
Be!
Free

Listen to me
I am who am
Freely free
I am who am is
Ever was
Ever shall be

No time in oneness
Oneness is

In the circle of love
There is no concept of time
Time free
Be free
In the circle of love
Be!

I am who am is
Be!

(1) - Sobhet - Deep Listening.
(2) - Jamal - Beauty, Jalal - Majesty.

25. A Handshake with the Invisible

Beloved of beloveds
The moment is this
The time is now
I am who am's presence
Is the meaning of now

I am who am is the silence one dwells in
Is the air one breathes
Is the essence of life
Is the meaning of life
Is the meaning of me
I am who am

I am who am is the essence of the human
I am who am is the gift of life
Is the kiss of earthly death

I am who am
Is
All that breathes
I am who am
Is
Be free

I am who am guides the feet
Shows the way
I am who am is the path
Is the way
I am who am is the feet
Is the map
Is the destination
Come play

The silent communication
The communication of of/in silence
Is sobhet (1)
Is the conversation of/in the heart of hearts

It is I am who am's silence
Taking flesh
It is I am who am's silence
Being professed
It is silence taking flesh

Before a thought is formed
Before a word is spoken
Before an action is taken
I am who am is
The silence of love and happiness
I am who am is
All else be

I am who am is a hidden treasure
Come look, listen
See
Be!

I am who am is closer to the human
Than the jugular vein
I am who am is the very air one breathes
I am who am is closer than the tear
Is to the eyelid

I am who am is
The heart of lovers
I am who am is the spark of life

Even as human flesh falls away
I am who am is
The forever in human time
In the timelessness
Of the timeless one

I am who am just is
Just is
Be!
Just is
Be!
Me
I am who am

A footprint of a miracle
A handshake with the invisible
Be!

I am who am
A speck of dust
Feet of clay
The word giveth
The lord taketh away
Blessed be
The nameless Lord

A new era is coming
A new time begun
For this is the reality of all
Under the sun

I am who am is always coming
I am who am always comes
Come

This is a time of decline for the human
As the human succumbs to its human frailty
When one gives one's heart over
To the landmines of the heart
How else could it be

Greed, hatred and ignorance
Also dwell in the silence

A shadow threatens to overcome
When the human hands its heart over to the shadows
Why is the human surprised
That s/he is overcome

Saying yes
Saying no
Is in the grasp of man

The human cannot claim ignorance
Once the light has shown
I am who am
Is
The light which has shown

Choose generosity over greed
Choose loving kindness over hatred
Choose wisdom over ignorance

Every tradition has been told
Every language has been spoken
Messages and messengers have been placed
In every earthly realm

It is up to the human
To walk
In her
In his
Place
Walk in I am who am's space

When the 'corruption' is from top to bottom
It does not leave much space
Invite others into silent fields
Call others into a silent place

Give them the tools to hear
To see
I am who am's voice
I am who am's face

I am who am is to be found
In the silence of the lord Buddha under a bo tree (1)
In the silence of a desert path
Where Jesus dwelt in me
I am who am

In a silent cave on the 27th night of Ramadan (2)
Where the prophet Mohammed first heard (3)
I am who am's
Voice

'Recite'
The prophet was told to say
It is in the same silence
124,000 messengers
Have been sent on their way

Sent to Be!
As much as sent to speak
Sent to be
A reflection of me
I am who am
In the mirrors of their hearts

Being-in-silence is the loudest voice spoken
Being-in-silence is when one's heart of hearts
Has been broken
Wide - open

Being-in-silence is a state of being
Is
The space
The place
The sphere
Where I am who am
Who am
Be!
Being-in-silence is
To be
Be!

*(1) - Bo tree - Bohdi Tree, sacred fig tree in India under which
Buddha gained enlightenment.*
*(2) - Ramadan - 9th month of the Islamic calendar. According to
Islamic belief, time for commemorating initial revelation of the
Koran to the prophet Mohammed.*
(3) - Prophet Mohammed - Founder of Islam.

26. Love Left Unspoken

In the mystery of oneness
In the mystery of me
There is only freedom
Freedom free

Touch this aspect of the mystery of me
I am who am
Touch the mystery freely
Be!
Free!

For in the mystery of oneness
How else could it be
Oneness is one
In freedom
Freely
Now
Be! Freedom freely

In the mystery of oneness
In the mystery of one
In the mystery of me
I am who am
Be!
Be the mystery in me

Freedom is freedom
Free freely

The human clings to its limitations
I am who am is freedom free
Be!
Freedom

Be!
Free
In oneness in me

Oneness in silence
Is
Oneness in one
Write freely

Oneness in silence
Is
Oneness in the sun
Oneness is oneness
In one

The sun always rises
Be one
The sun lies behind the clouds
Be one
The sun hides behind the veils
Be one

Behind the dim unknown lies God
Within the shadows
Keeping watch above her own
As Martin eloquently did say (1)

Beyond the darkness
Lies the light
Behind the dim unknown
Is the silence of the night

Beyond the treble greens
Within the darkest midnight
Lies I am who am

In silence
Silently keeping watch
Above her own
Every drop in the ocean is known to me
I am who am

When I am who am
Looks at the mountain
A million eye of mine
Stare back at me
Look at me
Look at me
Look only
At me

There are servants
Among I am's servants
Who love me and
I am who am loves them
A mystery in rhyme
Of a love left unspoken
I am who am
Is
Love
Left unspoken

In an early morning chant
I am who am speaks
Speaks out of the silence
Speaks to the proud
Speaks to the meek

It is I am who am
Who washes the feet
Be awashed in me
I am who am

Be the water which washes the feet of another
Be the towel which dries the feet
And sends the other to be on their way

I am who am is the feet
Is the water
Is the love
Is the lover
Is the beloved
It is all one in the eyes of I am who am

See the world with the eyes of oneness
See me
I am who am freely
Free others to see the reality
As it is
Reality as it is meant to be
This is to love freely

This is to touch the reality of me
I am who am
Love
Free
Love
Freely
Be!
Freedom
Free
That is how it is meant to be

Love
Love freely
In
Me
I am who am
Be!

(1) - Martin Luther - was an American civil rights advocate, doctor and Baptist Minister.

Glossary

Bhai-Sahib - Sahib means Elder Brother in Hindi. He was a Hindu Sufi who was taught by a Muslim Sufi guru.

Fana - The annihilation *(as in Sufism)* of the individual human will before the will of God.

Hallaj - Mansur al-Hallaj (c858 - 922) was a Persian mystic, revolution writer and teacher of Sufi. He is well known for his poetry, being accused of heresy and also for his final execution.

I am who am - In the book of Exodus *(Chapter 3, verse 14)* in the Bible *(Old Testament)* Moses confronts God who is in a Burning Bush. He asks God what he and the Israelites should call Him. God answered to call Him, 'I am who I am'.

Khidr - A mystical figure that some believe to be described in the Quran as a righteous servant of God possessing great wisdom or mystic knowledge. In Sufi tradition, Khidr has come to be known as one of those who receive illumination direct from God without human mediation.

Maha Ghosananda - Samdech Preah Maha Ghosananda *(May 23, 1913 - March 12, 2007)* was a highly revered Cambodian Buddhist monk in the Theravada tradition. He served as the Patriarch of Cambodian Buddhism during the Khmer Rouge and post-communist transition period of Cambodian history. His name means, 'great joyful proclaimer'. He was well known in Cambodia for his annual peace marches and was frequently referred to as the 'Ghandi' of Cambodia.

Oneness in God - In Christian belief there is a oneness with God the Father, through His Holy Spirit, living in the believer. Jesus said, 'On that day you will realise that I am in my Father, and you are in me, and I am in you' (John 14:20). In Muslim belief, every prophet preached the same main Islamic beliefs, the Oneness of God, worshipping of that one God, refraining from idolatry and sin, and the belief in the Day of Resurrection or the Day of Judgment and life after death.
The Sufi is on a mystical journey unveiling the oneness with God and aiming to be united with God.

Sihr - The Sihr were peaceful spiritual beings who led very simple lives.

Sobhet - A sobhet is being in communion with the Divine. It is one of three steps to relate to God. The first is prayer, the second meditation and the third sobhet.

Sufism - An Islamic belief in which Muslims seek divine knowledge and love through personal experience with God and to facilitate these in the world. Sufism is neither a religion nor a philosophy, but a way of life, as such anyone can become a Sufi.

124,000 - This number comes from a collection of the reports claiming to quote what the prophet Muhammed said on any matter called a 'hadith' in which the number of prophets was said to be 124,000.

About the Editor Dr Edwin Pugh

Edwin Pugh was a professor and consultant in palliative medicine. He also has a longstanding ongoing involvement with Cambodia. This began as a charity worker living and working with Khmer refugees on the Thai-Cambodia border 1990-1991. He continues to be actively involved in charity work in Cambodia through two charities. He is a patron of a medical charity Transform Healthcare Cambodia (**www.transformhealthcarecambodia.org.uk**) and a board member of Transform Asia (**www.transformasia.us**).

In his work with dying patients and their families, and with refugees, Edwin became acutely aware that they have much in common as they face hardships, suffering and the stark reality of dying. They question their mortality, reason for suffering, values, worth, purpose and inevitably their understanding of 'God' - or no God. Edwin's professional life was coloured by these profound experiences and he developed a specialist interest in spirituality, speaking and publishing on this issue.

A Movements Muffin

'Movements Muffins' are a new type of digital *(and sometimes a slim paperback/hardback)* book. They are aimed at readers on the move and are designed to tempt you to want to know more about a range of positive subjects. 'Muffins' are mainly, but not always, non-fiction.

So why not settle down with a coffee and a 'Muffin', and widen your horizons.

To discover more of our publications, check out our website, **www.movements.me.uk** periodically.

Fly Without a Shadow - Meditations on Oneness

Edited by Dr Edwin Pugh

Kindle ISBN - 978 1 898650 49 2

ePub ISBN - 978 1 898650 88 1

Paperback ISBN - 978 1 898650 89 8

Hardback ISBN - 978 1 898650 90 4

Part of the Movements Muffins 'Inspired Lives' Series

Also available by Dr Edwin Pugh is

Even The Crazy Man Wept – Reflections Following The War In Cambodia

www.ingramcontent.com/pod-product-compliance
Lightning Source LLC
Chambersburg PA
CBHW071534040426
42452CB00008B/1015